The Civics Test - 100 Questions & Answers for the Naturalization Test & U.S. Citizenship

Study guide with all 100 <u>official new</u> questions & answers!
(2022/2023/2024)

Written by RTB Education

Audiobook version narrated by Ron Garner.
Available to purchase on Audible & iTunes

The Civics Test

Table of Contents

Disclaimer	4
Copyright	5
Spanish Edition	6
Introduction	7
Chapter 1: Questions	9
Chapter 2: Answers	18
Chapter 3: Tips for Passing your Civics Test	31
Why the civics test is important..	31
Ten Tips for Passing the Civics Test:	32
Tips for the day of the exam:	36
Other parts of the path to citizenship:	36
Conclusion	38

Disclaimer

Please note the information contained within this document is for educational and entertainment purposes only. All effort has been executed to present accurate, up to date, and reliable, complete information. No warranties of any kind are declared or implied. Readers acknowledge that the author is not engaging in the rendering of legal, financial, medical or professional advice. The content within this book has been derived from various sources. Please consult a licensed professional before attempting any techniques outlined in this book.

By reading this document, the reader agrees that under no circumstances is the author responsible for any losses, direct or indirect, which are incurred as a result of the use of the information contained within this document, including, but not limited to, — errors, omissions, or inaccuracies.

Copyright

"This printed edition of the "The Civics Test - 100 Questions & Answers for the Naturalization Test & U.S. Citizenship" is a direct copy of the authentic work by the USCIS, produced with a new ISBN number to differentiate this book from the original work. The information presented in Civics Flash Cards for the Naturalization Test is considered public information and may be distributed or copied without alteration unless otherwise specified. Thus, the information and content within this book is cited from:

U.S. Department of Homeland Security, U.S. Citizenship and Immigration Services, Office of Citizenship, Civics Flash Cards for the Naturalization Test, Washington, D.C., 2019.

RTB Education

Spanish Edition

If you or somebody that you know, would prefer the Spanish edition of these civics test questions and answers - please go to Amazon or Audible and search "RTB Education" and you will find our Spanish version of this book.

Civics (History and Government) Questions for the Naturalization Test

Introduction

The 100 civics (history and government) questions and answers for the naturalization test are listed below. The civics test is an oral test and the USCIS Officer will ask the applicant up to 10 of the 100 civics questions. An applicant must answer 6 out of 10 questions correctly to pass the civics portion of the naturalization test. On the naturalization test, some answers may change because of elections or appointments. As you study for the test, make sure that you know the most current answers to these questions. Answer these questions with the name of the official who is serving at the time of your eligibility interview with USCIS. The USCIS Officer will not accept an incorrect answer.

*Although USCIS is aware that there may be additional correct answers to the 100 civics questions, applicants are encouraged to respond to the civics questions using the answers provided below.

**If you are 65 years old or older and have been a legal permanent resident of the United States for 20 or more years, you may study a fewer number of questions. For the list, go to www.uscis.gov

Please note - this is not a multiple-choice test, the answers given are each allowed answers to the questions. For example, sometimes there might be 3 possible answers to the same question.

Now, let's get to the questions and answers..

Chapter 1: Questions

*Write your answers on a separate piece of lined paper. Then once you've finished, check your answers at the back of the book.

AMERICAN GOVERNMENT
Part A: Principles of American Democracy

1. What is the supreme law of the land?

2. What does the Constitution do?

3. The idea of self-government is in the first three words of the Constitution. What are these words?

4. What is an amendment?

5. What do we call the first ten amendments to the Constitution?

6. What is one right or freedom from the First Amendment?*

7. How many amendments does the Constitution have?

8. What did the Declaration of Independence do?

9. What are two rights in the Declaration of Independence?

10. What is freedom of religion?

11. What is the economic system in the United States?*

12. What is the "rule of law"?

B: System of Government

13. Name one branch or part of the government.*

14. What stops one branch of government from becoming too powerful?

15. Who is in charge of the executive branch?

16. Who makes federal laws?

17. What are the two parts of the U.S. Congress?*

18. How many U.S. Senators are there?

19. We elect a U.S. Senator for how many years?

20. Who is one of your state's U.S. Senators now?*

21. The House of Representatives has how many voting members?

22. We elect a U.S. Representative for how many years?

23. Name your U.S. Representative.

24. Who does a U.S. Senator represent?

25. Why do some states have more Representatives than other states?

26. We elect a President for how many years?

27. In what month do we vote for President?*

28. What is the name of the President of the United States now?*

29. What is the name of the Vice President of the United States now?

30. If the President can no longer serve, who becomes President?

31. If both the President and the Vice President can no longer serve, who becomes President?

32. Who is the Commander in Chief of the military?

33. Who signs bills to become laws?

34. Who vetoes bills?

35. What does the President's Cabinet do?

36. What are two Cabinet-level positions?

37. What does the judicial branch do?

38. What is the highest court in the United States?

39. How many justices are on the Supreme Court?

40. Who is the Chief Justice of the United States now?

41. Under our Constitution, some powers belong to the federal government. What is one power of the federal government?

42. Under our Constitution, some powers belong to the states. What is one power of the states?

43. Who is the Governor of your state now?

44. What is the capital of your state?*

45. What are the two major political parties in the United States?*

46. What is the political party of the President now?

47. What is the name of the Speaker of the House of Representatives now?

C: Rights & Responsibilities

48. There are four amendments to the Constitution about who can vote. Describe one of them.

49. What is one responsibility that is only for United States citizens?*

50. Name one right only for United States citizens.

51. What are two rights of everyone living in the United States?

52. What do we show loyalty to when we say the Pledge of Allegiance?

53. What is one promise you make when you become a United States citizen?

54. How old do citizens have to be to vote for President?*

55. What are two ways that Americans can participate in their democracy?

56. When is the last day you can send in federal income tax forms?*

57. When must all men register for the Selective Service?

AMERICAN HISTORY
A: Colonial Period and Independence

58. What is one reason colonists came to America?

59. Who lived in America before the Europeans arrived?

60. What group of people was taken to America and sold as slaves?

61. Why did the colonists fight the British?

62. Who wrote the Declaration of Independence?

63. When was the Declaration of Independence adopted?

64. There were 13 original states. Name three.

65. What happened at the Constitutional Convention?

66. When was the Constitution written?

67. The Federalist Papers supported the passage of the U.S. Constitution. Name one of the writers.

68. What is one thing Benjamin Franklin is famous for?

69. Who is the "Father of Our Country"?

70. Who was the first President?*

The Civics Test

Part B: 1800s

71. What territory did the United States buy from France in 1803?

72. Name one war fought by the United States in the 1800s.

73. Name the U.S. war between the North and the South.

74. Name one problem that led to the Civil War.

75. What was one important thing that Abraham Lincoln did?*

76. What did the Emancipation Proclamation do?

77. What did Susan B. Anthony do?

78. Name one war fought by the United States in the 1900s.*

79. Who was President during World War I?

80. Who was President during the Great Depression and World War II?

81. Who did the United States fight in World War II?

82. Before he was President, Eisenhower was a general. What war was he in?

83. During the Cold War, what was the main concern of the United States?

84. What movement tried to end racial discrimination?

85. What did Martin Luther King, Jr. do?*

86. What major event happened on September 11, 2001, in the United States?

87. Name one American Indian tribe in the United States. [USCIS Officers will be supplied with a list of federally recognized American Indian tribes.]

INTEGRATED CIVICS A: Geography

88. Name one of the two longest rivers in the United States.

89. What ocean is on the West Coast of the United States?

90. What ocean is on the East Coast of the United States?

91. Name one U.S. territory.

92. Name one state that borders Canada.

93. Name one state that borders Mexico.

94. What is the capital of the United States?*

95. Where is the Statue of Liberty?*

B: Symbols

96. Why does the flag have 13 stripes?

97. Why does the flag have 50 stars?*

98. What is the name of the national anthem?

C: Holidays

99. When do we celebrate Independence Day?*

100. Name two national U.S. holidays.

Chapter 2: Answers

AMERICAN GOVERNMENT
Part A: Principles of American Democracy

1. What is the supreme law of the land? ▪ the Constitution

2. What does the Constitution do? ▪ sets up the government ▪ defines the government ▪ protects basic rights of Americans

3. The idea of self-government is in the first three words of the Constitution. What are these words? ▪ We the People

4. What is an amendment? ▪ a change (to the Constitution) ▪ an addition (to the Constitution)

5. What do we call the first ten amendments to the Constitution? ▪ the Bill of Rights

6. What is one right or freedom from the First Amendment?* ▪ speech ▪ religion ▪ assembly ▪ press ▪ petition the government

7. How many amendments does the Constitution have? ▪ twenty-seven (27)

8. What did the Declaration of Independence do? • announced our independence (from Great Britain) • declared our independence (from Great Britain) • said that the United States is free (from Great Britain)

9. What are two rights in the Declaration of Independence? • life • liberty • pursuit of happiness

10. What is freedom of religion? • You can practice any religion, or not practice a religion.

11. What is the economic system in the United States?* • capitalist economy • market economy

12. What is the "rule of law"? • Everyone must follow the law. • Leaders must obey the law. • Government must obey the law. • No one is above the law.

B: System of Government

13. Name one branch or part of the government.* • Congress • legislative • President • executive • the courts • judicial

14. What stops one branch of government from becoming too powerful? • checks and balances • separation of powers

15. Who is in charge of the executive branch? • the President

16. Who makes federal laws? ▪ Congress ▪ Senate and House (of Representatives) ▪ (U.S. or national) legislature

17. What are the two parts of the U.S. Congress?* ▪ the Senate and House (of Representatives)

18. How many U.S. Senators are there? ▪ one hundred (100)

19. We elect a U.S. Senator for how many years? ▪ six (6)

20. Who is one of your state's U.S. Senators now?* ▪ Answers will vary. [District of Columbia residents and residents of U.S. territories should answer that D.C. (or the territory where the applicant lives) has no U.S. Senators.]

21. The House of Representatives has how many voting members? ▪ four hundred thirty-five (435)

22. We elect a U.S. Representative for how many years? ▪ two (2)

23. Name your U.S. Representative. ▪ Answers will vary. [Residents of territories with nonvoting Delegates or Resident Commissioners may provide the name of that Delegate or Commissioner. Also acceptable is any statement that the territory has no (voting) Representatives in Congress.]

24. Who does a U.S. Senator represent? ▪ all people of the state

The Civics Test

25. Why do some states have more Representatives than other states? ▪ (because of) the state's population ▪ (because) they have more people ▪ (because) some states have more people

26. We elect a President for how many years? ▪ four (4)

27. In what month do we vote for President?* ▪ November

28. What is the name of the President of the United States now?* ▪ Visit uscis.gov/citizenship/testupdates for the name of the President of the United States. As we speak, it is Joe Biden in 2022.

29. What is the name of the Vice President of the United States now? ▪ Visit uscis.gov/citizenship/testupdates for the name of the Vice President of the United States.

30. If the President can no longer serve, who becomes President? ▪ the Vice President

31. If both the President and the Vice President can no longer serve, who becomes President? ▪ the Speaker of the House

32. Who is the Commander in Chief of the military? ▪ the President

33. Who signs bills to become laws? ▪ the President

34. Who vetoes bills? ▪ the President

35. What does the President's Cabinet do? • advises the President

36. What are two Cabinet-level positions? • Secretary of Agriculture • Secretary of Commerce • Secretary of Defense • Secretary of Education • Secretary of Energy • Secretary of Health and Human Services • Secretary of Homeland Security • Secretary of Housing and Urban Development • Secretary of the Interior • Secretary of Labor • Secretary of State • Secretary of Transportation • Secretary of the Treasury • Secretary of Veterans Affairs • Attorney General • Vice President

37. What does the judicial branch do? • reviews laws • explains laws • resolves disputes (disagreements) • decides if a law goes against the Constitution

38. What is the highest court in the United States? • the Supreme Court

39. How many justices are on the Supreme Court? • Visit uscis.gov/citizenship/testupdates for the number of justices on the Supreme Court.

40. Who is the Chief Justice of the United States now? • Visit uscis.gov/citizenship/testupdates for the name of the Chief Justice of the United States.

41. Under our Constitution, some powers belong to the federal government. What is one power of the federal government? • to print money • to declare war • to create an army • to make treaties

42. Under our Constitution, some powers belong to the states. What is one power of the states? ▪ provide schooling and education ▪ provide protection (police) ▪ provide safety (fire departments) ▪ give a driver's license ▪ approve zoning and land use

43. Who is the Governor of your state now? ▪ Answers will vary. [District of Columbia residents should answer that D.C. does not have a Governor.]

44. What is the capital of your state?* ▪ Answers will vary. [District of Columbia residents should answer that D.C. is not a state and does not have a capital. Residents of U.S. territories should name the capital of the territory.]

45. What are the two major political parties in the United States?* ▪ Democratic and Republican

46. What is the political party of the President now? ▪ Visit uscis.gov/citizenship/testupdates for the political party of the President.

47. What is the name of the Speaker of the House of Representatives now? ▪ Visit uscis.gov/citizenship/testupdates for the name of the Speaker of the House of Representatives.

C: Rights and Responsibilities

48. There are four amendments to the Constitution about who can vote. Describe one of them. ▪ Citizens eighteen (18) and older (can vote). ▪ You don't have to pay (a poll tax) to vote. ▪ Any citizen can vote. (Women and men can vote.) ▪ A male citizen of any race (can vote).

49. What is one responsibility that is only for United States citizens?* ▪ serve on a jury ▪ vote in a federal election

50. Name one right only for United States citizens. ▪ vote in a federal election ▪ run for federal office

51. What are two rights of everyone living in the United States? ▪ freedom of expression ▪ freedom of speech ▪ freedom of assembly ▪ freedom to petition the government ▪ freedom of religion ▪ the right to bear arms

52. What do we show loyalty to when we say the Pledge of Allegiance? ▪ the United States ▪ the flag

53. What is one promise you make when you become a United States citizen? ▪ give up loyalty to other countries ▪ defend the Constitution and laws of the United States ▪ obey the laws of the United States ▪ serve in the U.S. military (if needed) ▪ serve (do important work for) the nation (if needed) ▪ be loyal to the United States

54. How old do citizens have to be to vote for President?* ▪ eighteen (18) and older

The Civics Test

55. What are two ways that Americans can participate in their democracy? ▪ vote ▪ join a political party ▪ help with a campaign ▪ join a civic group ▪ join a community group ▪ give an elected official your opinion on an issue ▪ call Senators and Representatives ▪ publicly support or oppose an issue or policy ▪ run for office ▪ write to a newspaper

56. When is the last day you can send in federal income tax forms?* ▪ April 15

57. When must all men register for the Selective Service? ▪ at age eighteen (18) ▪ between eighteen (18) and twenty-six (26)

AMERICAN HISTORY
A: Colonial Period and Independence

58. What is one reason colonists came to America? ▪ freedom ▪ political liberty ▪ religious freedom ▪ economic opportunity ▪ practice their religion ▪ escape persecution

59. Who lived in America before the Europeans arrived? ▪ American Indians ▪ Native Americans

60. What group of people was taken to America and sold as slaves? ▪ Africans ▪ people from Africa

61. Why did the colonists fight the British? ▪ because of high taxes (taxation without representation) ▪ because the

British army stayed in their houses (boarding, quartering) ▪ because they didn't have self-government

62. Who wrote the Declaration of Independence? ▪ (Thomas) Jefferson

63. When was the Declaration of Independence adopted? ▪ July 4, 1776

64. There were 13 original states. Name three. ▪ New Hampshire ▪ Massachusetts ▪ Rhode Island ▪ Connecticut ▪ New York ▪ New Jersey ▪ Pennsylvania ▪ Delaware ▪ Maryland ▪ Virginia ▪ North Carolina ▪ South Carolina ▪ Georgia

65. What happened at the Constitutional Convention? ▪ The Constitution was written. ▪ The Founding Fathers wrote the Constitution.

66. When was the Constitution written? ▪ 1787

67. The Federalist Papers supported the passage of the U.S. Constitution. Name one of the writers. ▪ (James) Madison ▪ (Alexander) Hamilton ▪ (John) Jay ▪ Publius

68. What is one thing Benjamin Franklin is famous for? ▪ U.S. diplomat ▪ oldest member of the Constitutional Convention ▪ first Postmaster General of the United States ▪ writer of "Poor Richard's Almanac" ▪ started the first free libraries

69. Who is the "Father of Our Country"? ▪ (George) Washington

70. Who was the first President?* ▪ (George) Washington

Part B: 1800s

71. What territory did the United States buy from France in 1803? ▪ the Louisiana Territory ▪ Louisiana

72. Name one war fought by the United States in the 1800s. ▪ War of 1812 ▪ Mexican-American War ▪ Civil War ▪ Spanish-American War

73. Name the U.S. war between the North and the South. ▪ the Civil War ▪ the War between the States

74. Name one problem that led to the Civil War. ▪ slavery ▪ economic reasons ▪ states' rights

75. What was one important thing that Abraham Lincoln did?* ▪ freed the slaves (Emancipation Proclamation) ▪ saved (or preserved) the Union ▪ led the United States during the Civil War

76. What did the Emancipation Proclamation do? ▪ freed the slaves ▪ freed slaves in the Confederacy ▪ freed slaves in the Confederate states ▪ freed slaves in most Southern states

77. What did Susan B. Anthony do? ▪ fought for women's rights ▪ fought for civil rights C: Recent American History and Other Important Historical Information

78. Name one war fought by the United States in the 1900s.* ▪ World War I ▪ World War II ▪ Korean War ▪ Vietnam War ▪ (Persian) Gulf War

79. Who was President during World War I? ▪ (Woodrow) Wilson

80. Who was President during the Great Depression and World War II? ▪ (Franklin) Roosevelt

81. Who did the United States fight in World War II? ▪ Japan, Germany, and Italy

82. Before he was President, Eisenhower was a general. What war was he in? ▪ World War II

83. During the Cold War, what was the main concern of the United States? ▪ Communism

84. What movement tried to end racial discrimination? ▪ civil rights (movement)

85. What did Martin Luther King, Jr. do?* ▪ fought for civil rights ▪ worked for equality for all Americans

86. What major event happened on September 11, 2001, in the United States? ▪ Terrorists attacked the United States.

87. Name one American Indian tribe in the United States. [USCIS Officers will be supplied with a list of federally recognized American Indian tribes.] ▪ Cherokee ▪ Navajo ▪ Sioux ▪ Chippewa ▪ Choctaw ▪ Pueblo ▪ Apache ▪ Iroquois

- Creek - Blackfeet - Seminole - Cheyenne - Arawak - Shawnee - Mohegan - Huron - Oneida - Lakota - Crow - Teton - Hopi - Inuit

INTEGRATED CIVICS A:
Geography

88. Name one of the two longest rivers in the United States.
- Missouri (River) - Mississippi (River)

89. What ocean is on the West Coast of the United States? - Pacific (Ocean)

90. What ocean is on the East Coast of the United States? - Atlantic (Ocean)

91. Name one U.S. territory. - Puerto Rico - U.S. Virgin Islands - American Samoa - Northern Mariana Islands - Guam

92. Name one state that borders Canada. - Maine - New Hampshire - Vermont - New York - Pennsylvania - Ohio - Michigan - Minnesota - North Dakota - Montana - Idaho - Washington - Alaska

93. Name one state that borders Mexico. - California - Arizona - New Mexico - Texas

94. What is the capital of the United States?* - Washington, D.C.

95. Where is the Statue of Liberty?* ▪ New York (Harbor) ▪ Liberty Island [Also acceptable are New Jersey, near New York City, and on the Hudson (River).]

B: Symbols

96. Why does the flag have 13 stripes? ▪ because there were 13 original colonies ▪ because the stripes represent the original colonies

97. Why does the flag have 50 stars?* ▪ because there is one star for each state ▪ because each star represents a state ▪ because there are 50 states

98. What is the name of the national anthem? ▪ The Star-Spangled Banner

C: Holidays

99. When do we celebrate Independence Day?* ▪ July 4

100. Name two national U.S. holidays. ▪ New Year's Day ▪ Martin Luther King, Jr. Day ▪ Presidents' Day ▪ Memorial Day ▪ Independence Day ▪ Labor Day ▪ Columbus Day ▪ Veterans Day ▪ Thanksgiving ▪ Christmas

Chapter 3: Tips for Passing your Civics Test

Why the civics test is important..

The questions and knowledge that you're questioned about in the civics test are mostly related to American History & Government. These are important things to know as a member of American society. They will allow you to feel at home, as for example on the 4th of July (Independence Day) - you'll understand what everybody is celebrating, as opposed to not understanding why everybody seems to be throwing a party at the same time!

By understanding the content inside this test, you'll have more understanding of the history of this country, and the American people will be happy to have you as an outstanding and commendable member of society.

It's important that you learn all the questions and answers for the civics test, because you only get 2 opportunities to take the exam. If you fail twice (by scoring less than 6/10), you will not be granted U.S. Citizenship.

Before we get to the ten tips, let's quickly look at some recent statistics about naturalization, and the people that succeeded in becoming citizens of the United States in one recent year…

Despite the pandemic, in the fiscal year 2020, the US accepted over 625,000 new citizens. The countries where most people came from included, in order, Mexico, India, The Philippines, Cuba & China. These people moved to many different cities, but the most popular were Miami, Brooklyn, Houston, the Bronx, and Las Vegas. There were more women than Men, 18% of them were younger than 30, and a few were even older than 100! Wow!

This demonstrates that anybody can become a citizen of the USA, and should inspire you with confidence! With enough hard work, you'll make it happen.

Just for your reference, if you pass - your naturalization application may be approved on the same day - or it could take up to 120 days for them to make a decision. Once accepted, you will do a ceremony to take an oath of allegiance, get your certificate, and then you will be a united states citizen.

Ten Tips for Passing the Civics Test:

In this part, we'll give you ten tips for passing the civics test. These are things you might not have previously known.

1) If you fail the exam the first time, you'll have a gap of around 60 days in order to pass your test the next time around. Use this time to your advantage and ensure that you succeed the second time around.

2) Practice your English listening and speaking skills. Because the civics test is an oral exam - it's crucial to understand which question is actually being asked - and therefore, you'll know how to answer it. To practice your English, use websites like Duolingo, and converse with people online, on zoom calls, at the grocery store, etc. Find any opportunity you can to converse your spoken English - and you'll find the exam easier. Another good idea is to watch films and tv in English, as you will unconsciously become more fluent as you watch. A further thing to do is to read books in English, whether these are fiction, non-fiction or even kids' books - these things will help to improve your reading, writing and speaking - which is important in other parts of the naturalization test, which we will talk about in a moment.

3) Take practice tests - Here on the US Government Website, (https://www.uscis.gov/citizenship-resource-center/find-study-materials-and-resources/study-for-the-test-2008-version/2008-civics-practice-test) you'll find practice tests. The more you do, the more confident you'll feel when it comes to the day of your test. It will feel like a real exam, so treat it like one and give it your best.

4) Split up your studying by topic. Did you know that this test is split into multiple sections, for example: Principles of American Democracy, System of Government, Rights & Responsibilities, American History (which is further split into colonial, 1800's and recent history), Geography, Symbols &

Holidays. If you identify, for example, that you are failing the most questions in the history section, it would be wise to spend more time focusing on that, compared to focusing on the other sections - until you are equally good at all of them. This will allow you to have a well-rounded understanding of America & the answers you must give to pass the exam.

5) Use other material - Use everything at your disposal - While we think that memorizing these answers will be sufficient - there are many other ways to practice for the civics test - such as apps on the app store & google store. There is also an app by the government, in which you can practice questions, and see your progress over time. There are also other books available on Amazon.

6) Get somebody else to test you - Another great way to study is to ask a family member, friend or work colleague to test you on some questions. This is a really great way to practice because it will feel like a closer experience to the real exam, where the officer will be asking you your 10 questions.

7) Watch the news and read the newspapers - While normally we don't advise to watch the news (in most countries it is very negative and depressing), if you are preparing for the civics test - it's vital that you know the current events in the economy. The reason for this is that you'll possibly be asked questions about who the current president is, who the current vice-president is, and other time relevant questions such as who the speaker of the house of representatives is. You'll have noticed

some of these questions above. Therefore, if you don't keep up to date with current day to day events in the USA, you might get these wrong. So, here, no matter how negative the news can seem, the news is very important to follow!

8) Don't doubt yourself - Many test takers spend too much time doubting themselves, and not enough time believing in themselves. Remember, the dictionary definition of humble is meek, or having or showing a modest or low estimate of one's importance. It's better to be confident in your skills, if you've done the hard work to back it up.

9) Stay calm - Be sure to use everything at your disposal to stay calm. If you are a person with a nervous personality when it comes to test taking, then you should do everything you can to be as calm as possible on the day. This could include things such as doing breathing exercises, breathing deeply in out and out slowly. It could also include some exercise before the test, to work out any stress out of your body.

10) Have Fun - The final tip is to have fun. This might sound hard when you are nervous - but once you have passed you will likely look back on this whole process with nostalgia. A positive and happy outlook will serve you much better than thinking you will fail.

Tips for the day of the exam:

On the day of your exam, it is important to get there early. Make sure you have had a good, reliable breakfast. Make sure to drink enough water, but not too much. For me, the best brain-food on the day of an exam is always to eat some wheat cereal with a little sugar. This slow-release energy will mean that you have enough energy, but do not crash. If you need a coffee or tea, don't go overboard - as too much could make you anxious and therefore you might not perform at your best.

Like we said, make sure you get to where you need to be well ahead of time. Please don't be late, so account for any traffic or public transport delays. This will also leave you feeling more relaxed.

Other parts of the path to citizenship:

There are two other parts to the citizenship test. These include:

The English Reading & Writing Test - In this part, you'll need to demonstrate your understanding of the English language through reading, writing, and speaking. In the reading and writing part, you will use an iPad or similar device - this will be provided to you so you will not need to buy one.

The Civics Test

For the reading section, you will be asked to read sentences from the iPad, to demonstrate your reading skills.

In the speaking part, the officer will ask you questions such as "where were you born" or "how long have you been in the United States".

In the writing part, some of the vocabulary words (which follow) will be included. The writing vocabulary words can be found here: https://www.uscis.gov/sites/default/files/document/guides/writing_vocab.pdf . During the writing section, the officer will say a sentence, which you then write down on the iPad. To pass this aspect, you'll need to get 1 out of 3 sentences correct. Remember to look at the vocabulary list as some of the words may be from here. When it comes to numbers, you can write these as numbers instead of words if you like, however you shouldn't abbreviate words.

The Vocabulary Test - In this part, you'll need to know some common words in the English language. A list of vocabulary to know can be found here: https://www.uscis.gov/sites/default/files/document/guides/reading_vocab.pdf. The vocabulary lists include American themed words like Independence Day, and verbs like "vote", "can", & "want".

We wish you the best of luck for your civics and naturalization test, & with good practice - we are confident that you will be extremely successful in passing the test and obtaining your U.S. Citizenship.

Conclusion

That brings us to the end of the questions and answers. You can use this book as many times as you need until you consistently score above 60% when taking practice tests.

Remember, during the test, the USCIS Officer will ask you up to 10 of the 100 civics questions. An applicant must answer 6 out of 10 questions correctly to pass the civics portion of the naturalization test. On the naturalization test, some answers may change because of elections or appointments. As you study for the test, make sure that you know the most current answers to these questions. Answer these questions with the name of the official who is serving at the time of your eligibility interview with USCIS. The USCIS Officer will not accept an incorrect answer.

*Although USCIS is aware that there may be additional correct answers to the 100 civics questions, applicants are encouraged to respond to the civics questions using the answers provided below.

Spanish Edition
If you, or somebody you know - would prefer the Spanish edition of these civics test questions and answers - please go to Audible and search "RTB Education" and you will find our Spanish version of this book.

Thank you for reading "The Civics Test - 100 Questions & Answers for the Naturalization Test & U.S. Citizenship, written by RTB Education & audiobook edition narrated by Ron Garner.

Please leave a 5* on Amazon review if you enjoyed and found this book useful.

www.ingramcontent.com/pod-product-compliance
Lightning Source LLC
Chambersburg PA
CBHW012014090526
44590CB00026B/3999